MW00776188

Obsessed with Your Phone?

Disconnecting to Connect

William P. Smith

New Growth Press

WWW.NEWGROWTHPRESS.COM

New Growth Press, Greensboro, NC 27404
www.newgrowthpress.com
Copyright © 2018 by William P. Smith

Scripture quotations are taken from THE HOLY BIBLE, NEW
INTERNATIONAL VERSION®, NIV®, copyright © 1973,
1978, 1984, 2011 by Biblica, Inc.® Used by permission. All
rights reserved worldwide.

Cover Design: Faceout Books, faceoutstudio.com
Typesetting and eBook: Lisa Parnell, lparnell.com

ISBN: 978-1-948130-36-3 (Print)
ISBN: 978-1-948130-35-6 (eBook)

Library of Congress Cataloging-in-Publication Data on File

Printed in China

25 24 23 22 21 20 19 18   1 2 3 4 5

Kayla woke up to her smartphone's alarm, shut it off, then opened up several apps. Bleary-eyed and struggling to focus, she spot-checked her social media accounts, scanned the news, then the weather, and looked through her calendar, all before getting out of bed.

Throughout the rest of the day, her phone would be her constant companion, never more than arm's length away. She chose clips from a comedian during breakfast, listened to music on her way into work, glanced at alerts and pop-up messages at her desk throughout the day, responded to texts and email during meetings, and monitored the progress of the stock market.

She played a few rounds of the latest game she was hooked on in the ladies' room, took a call while at lunch with her friend, zoned out to a couple of talking heads on the way home, and binge-watched her latest series before turning out the light—all while constantly monitoring her friends' lives and posting about her own. Her phone barely made it to the nightstand before she nodded off.

At this point in time, Kayla cannot imagine life without it.

Can you see yourself in Kayla? I know I do—maybe more than I'd like to admit. On any given day I might be more than a little uncomfortable if you asked me, "Do you own your smartphone, or does it own you?"

Here's a quiz to help you decide how you would answer that same question:

- How quickly do you pick up your phone in the morning? Do you hear from it before you hear from God?
- Do you check your phone multiple times a day (or hour) to make sure you know what's going on in the world and with your friends?
- Can you usually see or feel your phone?
- Does it spend more time face up or face down when you're not carrying it?
- Do you find yourself turning to it first when you're sad, before you reach out to anyone else to comfort you?
- Does it entertain you when you have time you don't know what to do with? Distract you when you're upset? Calm you when you're angry?
- Do you misplace your phone less often than you do your keys?
- Have you ever picked up your phone to check an alert, only to find yourself coming back up for air from social media or the Internet an hour or so later?

It's amazing how quickly such a relatively new device has taken over so much of daily life for so many of us. The good news is: You don't have to throw yours away to get your life back. Let me first discuss why we find them so consuming, examine how they fit into God's world, and then point to a number of things you can do so that you end up owning your phone, rather than vice versa.

Why Do Our Phones Consume Us?

We use our phones to soothe ourselves when irritated, confused, anxious, bored, or upset—by playing games, seeing what our friends are doing or saying, catching up on the latest shows, or posting our complaints and frustrations. For many of us, they're the first thing we check in the morning and the last thing we look at before going to sleep— they've become such a constant companion that a significant percentage of people even sleep with them.[1] To underline the point that many people now turn to phones for companionship and connectedness, one man in Las Vegas literally married his.[2]

The amount of time we spend on our phones, however, does not produce greater personal or communal health. As screen time increases, people are more distracted, less skilled at engaging others face-to-face, feel increasingly isolated and alone, and are at greater risk of suicide.[3] And while you might think that someone would only engage in more screen time if it made them happier, the opposite is true. The reasons vary—seeing friends doing things without them, not getting as much affirmation for their posts as they hoped, being targeted by cyberbullies, or ending up depressed or anxious due to a lack of sleep—but the correlation is consistent: Greater screen time results in greater unhappiness.[4]

Despite the negative results, a frequently cited study noted that people reached for their phones around 150 times per day.[5] Another study, a few years later, discovered that on average we touch our screens—tapping, typing, swiping, or clicking—an incredible 2,617 times per day, and that the heaviest ten percent of users nearly double that rate, clocking in at 5,427 times.[6] Perhaps even more interesting than the vast amount of time we give to our devices is that when people hear those numbers, they seem relatively unconcerned.[7]

These effects prompt people to issue dire warnings that liken using your phone to ingesting candy laced with cyanide, or suggest that using technology is akin to drug use.[8] Less alarmist but more alarming are the tech designers who limit their own or their family's access to smartphones and tablets—devices they helped develop—because they're convinced of the dangers associated with becoming habitual users.[9]

Why, despite their harmful side effects, have these devices become so important to us so quickly? And what should we do if we recognize that we are becoming—or have become—obsessed with our phones?

The answer is multifaceted.

Voices from inside the tech industry claim that your phone's software plays a significant role. It is written to both grab and hold your attention, using the principle that randomly distributed rewards reinforce patterns of behavior. Designers code apps that keep you turning back to them, fueling an addictive compulsion to check your phone and recheck it and check some more.[10]

We look to see what's new in the world or what's going on with our friends. We want to see if anyone's liked what we posted or noticed how clever or right or creative we were. Anything new triggers a little pleasant chemical release in our brains that gives a little comfort, a little relief, a little delight, a little high, and so we compulsively keep coming back for more.[11]

The addiction to our phones stems from more than biochemical responses, however. As human beings, we're made in the image of God. We're social creatures who, in reflecting the society of the Trinity, want to stay connected with others. We're mini-rulers tasked to oversee this world, who need to know what's happening around us so that we know how to engage our communities well. We're mini-creators who design and develop better ideas when sharing dinner recipes, investment strategies, home remodeling ideas, and vacation plans. Even in the most benign context, you could easily be absorbed by what the Internet provides, given the nature of who you are as an image-bearer of God.

Sadly, since we live in an imperfect world and are imperfect people, we also use technology to pursue corrupted things such as pornography, the dark web, schemes that con the naïve, or videos that invite us to mock others made in the image of God—things that will not help us love God or those around us. Why would you pursue something destructive to yourself or others? Because you feel a hunger deep inside that you hope this pursuit, twisted though it is, will feed your soul.

Worse, however: That inner hunger leads us to engage even good things in an unhealthy way, because we never feel like we've had enough. And so we compulsively click, swipe, and tap, trying to convince ourselves that we're in the know; that we're liked, noticed, and wanted; that our contributions are valued—or, if none of that is currently satisfying, we'll settle for entertainment that numbs the emptiness.

Our engagement with unlimited access to an unlimited Internet is not a one-dimensional issue, nor is it restricted to any one population or social demographic or clustered in any one geographical location. It literally affects billions of people around the globe. In that sense you can say, without hyperbole, that it is taking place on an unprecedented scale. The warnings are dire and the stakes are high. So what do we do with this challenge?

How Do Smartphones Fit into God's World?

To answer that, we first need to ask, "How does God view things like technology?" Technological devices—smartphones, tablets, laptops—are part of creation that extend the power and influence of the human beings who design and use them.

But by using someone else's technological creation, you invite yourself to be shaped—influenced—by the device's creator who can't help but build their values into it. Those values, mediated through technology, incline you to prioritize certain things over others (i.e., if the designer's goal is to capture your attention, then you will learn to be more focused on your screen than you are on the quality of your human interactions). In that sense, technology is never neutral in its impact on human beings.

And yet it's also wrong to claim that every technology is inherently evil simply because it has unwanted or potentially destructive consequences. Rather, it depends on how and why it's used—either to dominate and destroy the human spirit or to liberate and empower human beings, to extend their influence in this world further than they otherwise could.

At its most basic, then, technology is one aspect of the inanimate creation that God chose humans to rule over—not to exploit it, but to care for it and work it like he would (Genesis 1:26–28; 2:15).

Sadly, our first ancestors chose a different path. They decided to use creation to serve their own purposes and throw off God's authority (Genesis 3:5–7). Their rebellion resulted in a physical world that's so badly broken that now every part of it—including your smartphone—has brokenness built into it (Romans 8:20–22).

The encouraging news is that because Jesus came to destroy the power of sin and reverse the curse of brokenness, you and I now have resources from Christ to engage a ruined creation—resources that we didn't have before coming to know him. You can approach technology optimistically, believing that you don't have to give in to misusing it. You now have the power to rule over it, but you will have to practice using the power Christ won for you in his death and resurrection.

How do you do that with your phone? Let me suggest several things that will help.

Godly Ways to Engage Your Phone

First, you need to understand what keeps you coming back for more. What's at the bottom of our inability to resist the pressures of smartphone technology? It's because we're looking for something from creation to satisfy an acute spiritual hunger we feel, but it's a hunger that has grown larger than what God intended.

While each person has their own particular hunger and ways of trying to fill it, we also share similarities with each other. Here are four common longings that will drive you to misuse your phone when they're out of control.

1. Searching for Significance. Your life matters. By virtue of being made in God's image, you are important and are supposed to be noticed, not taken for granted, but appreciated. You should be valued, not ignored. All of those are reasonable desires.

But those desires become unhealthy when it's not simply nice to be noticed, but you feel that it's necessary—essential, even. Combine that longing for attention with the use of your phone and you'll find yourself regularly checking your social media feeds to see:

- Did you get any new friend requests?
- Has anyone "liked" what you posted since the last time you checked?
- Have more people liked your post than your previous posts, or are your overall likes going down?
- Do you need to put up something more attention-grabbing to recapture them? Say something controversial? Share a slightly provocative picture?

When these kinds of questions drive you, you're no longer trying to connect with people. Instead you're measuring your worth and value by how much they notice you. You've transformed Socrates's dictum that "The unexamined life is not worth living" into "The unobserved life is not worth living."

The antidote is to remember that God sees you—all of you, not just the appealing parts that you choose to share. He sees you and loves you and through Jesus he's cleansed you (Genesis 16:11–13; Exodus 2:25; Matthew 9:35–36; Luke 15:20). You have his enthusiastic, wholehearted attention, despite having worked so hard to push him away (Zephaniah 3:17). If no one else noticed you or wanted to connect with you today, you have more than you need already.

2. Fear of Missing Out. Alternatively, you might not want to be noticed so much as you can't stand the thought of being left out. Maybe you're afraid that while you weren't online, your friends posted things or that something happened in the larger world that you don't know about—and now you feel like an outsider, trying to catch up.

Have you ever thought up and posted a really cool comment on someone's thread, only to discover that you were a day late and so you clicked furiously, trying to delete it before the other person or their community noticed?

That feeling of embarrassment comes because the accessibility of the medium makes it feel like there's no reason we shouldn't be constantly up to date. We get tired of saying, "Um, no, I didn't know that," and so the unspoken logic urges, "If I'm current with my friends, then I can never be surprised or embarrassed." And yet the volume of people engaging each other at all times of day and night means that we'll only be current if we are as constantly engaged as everyone else combined.

Here's the good news of the gospel: You can't miss out—at least, not on anything that will impact your life for eternity. You are not omniscient, all-knowing—and God doesn't expect you to be. It's appropriate as a human being—godly, even—to say, "No, I had no idea. Can you fill me in?" He has given his life to guarantee you a front-and-center seat to what he's doing. If something is truly important, he'll make sure you know about it.

3. Feeling Secure. Maybe for you, the virtual world provides a place that you can master. You can go where you want, when you want, for as long as you want, to do what you want. There are no restrictions, no rules—and if you prefer, no accountability. You are in charge of what you experience, and if you don't like something or it no longer suits you, you can go somewhere else with seemingly no repercussions. You craft the world that you want to live in.

How many people throughout time and history could lay claim to such a world? And yet, it's at your fingertips—merely one swipe or keystroke away—and it obeys your every command. That's a world that's hard to resist—a world that insulates you from having to deal with anything that you don't like or that makes you uncomfortable. Can you see why you'd go there often and be reluctant to leave?

Again, this calls for a big gospel; and again, what God offers is up to the challenge. Why insulate yourself from the difficulties of this world when God vows to use every experience you have, good or bad, to produce in you a fitness for his kingdom (Romans 8:28–30)?

The real world is a scary world and you have probably had at least your share of suffering in it. But if God transforms those experiences into glory that's beyond your ability to imagine (Romans 8:18), then to guard yourself from dealing with what he allows into your life is to cheat yourself.

Thankfully, he loves you too much to let you cut yourself out of glory—and will pursue you in the real world, even if you try escaping into a virtual one.

4. Being Entertained. In 1991, Bill Watterson drew a cartoon of a boy, Calvin, racing to a TV set, plopping himself down in front of it and demanding of it, "Pander to me!"[12] While neatly capturing in three words the human heart's demand to be entertained, the TV of Watterson's day was woefully inadequate by our standards. It could only offer a limited range of prepackaged, noninteractive programs at specified, fixed intervals. What would Watterson's Calvin say today?

Likely the same thing, since time doesn't change our hearts. It just offers a bigger variety of options. From videos to games to newsfeeds to personal time-lines through which you can scroll endlessly, you can spend as much time as you have since your heart doesn't tire of demanding, "I must be indulged!" What could be better?

What *is* better is the way Jesus restores the goodness of work. What's better is the recovery of work, not as toil and labor (Genesis 3:17–19), but as a delight, because it is central to you as an image of God—you're a worker because you reflect the Master Worker (compare Genesis 1:1–27 with Genesis 1:28; 2:15). This is a small part of your identity that Christ's redemption wins back for you.

And so you neither elevate work above rest—nor just as importantly, rest above work. Rather, you reject a world vacillating between the extremes of workaholism and self-indulgence, because you've been embraced by a God who both works and rests (Genesis 2:2–3). That's the same God who adopts you and raises you to love the things that he loves. And as his child, you learn to agree with him that it's a good thing to work—to create, to build, to shape, to move, to organize—for six days and then to rest one, rather than indulge yourself as often as you possibly can.

Identifying your unique temptations is important, but that's not the same as relying on the gospel. The gospel of Jesus Christ is only wonderful if you apply it and live by it. Otherwise, it's useless. Living the Christian life, then, is more than an intellectual exercise, more than simply a shift in your thinking.

To live out the gospel, start by meditating on what Christ's death and resurrection mean for one of the four areas above that tempt you. Go back and consider what he has done for you and the kind of life he's now made possible for you to have. Then meditate on those twin realities—turn them over and over in your mind—until both he and that new way of living become more real and beautiful than what you used to believe would satisfy your soul.

But let me warn you: When you start focusing on him and his way of living, it may feel like you're going backwards, as you see how strongly you're tempted by your desires and how little you want to resist. Take heart: You're now seeing what you hadn't. Those new glimpses of the depth of your need are one sign that you're growing.

When you see your need, run back to Jesus, asking for both his forgiveness and his strength to turn away from them again. Do that and you'll see yourself overcoming temptation one small step at a time, as you experience the truth that "the one who is in you is greater than the one who is in the world" (1 John 4:4). It takes effort, but you can grow in your ability to fight temptation by the power of the Holy Spirit inside of you.

Understanding how you can be led astray is your first step, but it's not your last. As anyone will tell you who has had to learn godly ways of engaging creation, there are things you will need to stop doing and things you need to begin doing.

Take eating habits, as an example. Is there anybody who has never struggled with how and what they eat? There is a healthy kind of saying "No" to some foods and amounts, while actively saying "Yes" to others. Neither of those is easy. Both take time and practice, and include many fails and retries.

Learning to use your phone wisely is similar. You're going to need to limit how and how often you use it, while at the same time becoming very deliberate about why you pick it up when you do. Let's consider the limitations side first.

Restraint, setting limits and boundaries, self-control—these are the skills you need to develop so that you are not mastered by anything in creation, including your phone (1 Corinthians 6:12). They're also words that aren't immediately attractive to many people; they run counter to our natural inclination to indulge ourselves. Let's see if we can glimpse something more positive about these skills by setting them within the context of the Sabbath principle, since the Sabbath was designed for our good (Mark 2:27).

The Sabbath is both a restorative day (Exodus 20:11) and a day to remind yourself that God doesn't need your constant participation in his world in order to keep it going (Deuteronomy 5:15). A healthy part of engaging any aspect of his world, then, involves regularly resting from it—to be personally refreshed and refueled while not being mastered by it. While Sabbath clearly takes place on a weekly cycle, it's also healthy to build in daily, mini-Sabbath rhythms as well.

So what does it look like practically to Sabbath from our phones?

- The easiest thing you can do is turn off all unnecessary alerts and updates. When your phone calls to you less often, you will be less absorbed by it.
- In the same way that a bathroom scale provides a measurable reality check when you're wrestling with what you're eating, it might help you to see how much time and energy you already invest in your phone. Consider downloading an app that will monitor and report your daily usage. If you're like most people, you'll be surprised at how often you're on your phone.
- Next, determine what you think is a reasonable amount of time to give to newsfeeds, articles, blogs, videos, and social media. Then get an app that will let you know when you've reached or exceeded your limit. Alternatively: Why not

enlist several friends, who you can be accountable to daily for how much you used it, while you're retraining yourself?

- It's easy to say, "Don't keep checking your phone," but what are you supposed to do instead? And how do you keep from missing something important? Think more proactively. Decide what important times throughout the day would be good for you to check your phone, and practice limiting your usage to those times. You'll still be available if someone needs to contact you outside of those times, but you won't be drawn in as easily as when you don't have specific times in mind. And just like a child who can't govern itself but needs to rest anyway, give your phone a set "bedtime" when you plug it in, and leave it until the next day.

- Set up phone-free zones in your home, so that portable electronics can't intrude into all areas of your life. For instance, don't allow any phone at the dinner table or when you're playing a game with friends or family, except in extreme emergencies. Train yourself to place your phone face down when you're with people, as a reminder to yourself to focus more on them. And don't allow your phone in your bedroom. Buy an alarm clock, if necessary!

- Lastly, consider giving yourself regular media fasts. Unplug yourself for at least a day each week or month, or even perhaps a week each year from all electronics. In the same way that fasting from food reminds you to hunger for the ultimate source of life, fasting from your phone can remind you to do the same thing. Just make sure that when you feel the cravings for attention, being included, feeling secure, or being entertained that you turn to the Lord and ask him to fill you instead.

In other words, if your soul is hungry, feed it. Spend time with the Lord—not as an escape and not so that he'll give you what you crave in the same way that your phone will, but because there is nothing on earth that can take his place. Practice a friendship with the Lord that leaves you hungering for "updates" and "statuses" from him more than you do from your phone.

Now, if you've ever tried to break a bad habit, you already know that it's much easier when you're focused on what you want to build into your life more than on what you're trying to eliminate from it. Since the danger of a smartphone is that it pulls you in and absorbs you, you'll need to learn to use it intentionally and deliberately. But to what end? So that it lets you connect better with other images of God, rather than isolating you from them. Here are a few ideas of what that might look like:

- Instead of aimlessly searching the Internet for something to interest you or wandering through your contacts' social media, decide that you're going to use your phone to reach out to someone. Take a moment to think of who you can text to brighten up their day. Or, if you have longer, identify someone you've not spoken to in a while and give them a call. At the worst, you'll leave them a voicemail, but even that will help rekindle a relationship that's been drifting apart.
- When you're reading what someone has posted, don't simply "like" it. Instead, compose a quick comment that inserts a personal element into the interaction—either something that lets you affirm them in some concrete manner or that lets you share something of yourself.
- Take a moment and realize that your friends are opening up ways for you to care for them better, given the wealth of information they're disclosing about themselves. As you're scrolling, ask yourself, "Is there a need I'm hearing that I can meet? Is there something that I could say to encourage them, support them, commiserate with them, or point them to what's helped me?"

At the very least, they're telling you how to pray for them, so take thirty seconds and do so, then reach out and tell them that you did. In other words, when you pick up your phone, think to yourself, "Here's an opportunity to minister and to serve." That mindset will change what you do, and where you go while you're on it.

- Lastly, the purpose of our sharing is not to call attention to ourselves as much as it is to love the Lord our God with everything we've got, and to love our neighbor as ourselves. The Internet redefines where those neighbors live physically, but the call to caring for them hasn't changed. Be thoughtful about what you post to your own social media accounts, by running it through the grid of Ephesians 4:29. Ask yourself, "Is what I'm posting:
   – helpful for building others up?
   – concerned for what others need to hear?
   – aimed at benefitting those who listen?"

   If what you want to say passes that threefold test, you'll have greater confidence that you're using your phone in a way that honors God— the one who has called you to live a life of faith in this century, with its own unique resources and challenges.

The nexus of the Internet—with its unlimited information, entertainment, and social media—and its easy access through portable electronic devices produces an enticing, compelling environment that is a challenge to manage or pull away from. And yet it was precisely for such challenges that Jesus died and rose again. What he did set you free from the power of sin and gave you everything you need to live a godly life that honors him and cares for the people around you. That high and lofty calling happens one click, tap, swipe, and keystroke at a time. Use each one well!

Endnotes

1. Bank of America, *Trends in Consumer Mobility Report*, http://newsroom.bankofamerica.com/files/doc_library /additional/2015_BAC_Trends_in_Consumer_Mobility_ Report.pdf (accessed 1/19/2018).

2. Erica Tempesta, "'In 18 months, he'll upgrade!' Man marries his SMARTPHONE in a bizarre Las Vegas ceremony to prove how 'precious phones have become in our daily lives," DailyMail.com, June 29, 2016, http://www.dailymail .co.uk/femail/article-3666133/In-18-months-ll-upgrade-Man-marries-SMARTPHONE-bizarre-Las-Vegas-ceremony -prove-precious-phones-daily-lives.html (accessed 1/19/2018).

3. Jean M. Twenge, "Have Smartphones Destroyed a Generation?" *The Atlantic*, September 2017, https:// www.theatlantic.com/magazine/archive/2017/09/has-the-smartphone-destroyed-a-generation/534198 (accessed 1/17/ 2018); Tristan Harris, "How Better Tech Could Protect Us from Distraction," *TED.com*, https://www.ted.com/talks /tristan_harris_how_better_tech_could_protect_us_from_ distraction (accessed 1/17/2018).

4. Twenge, "Have Smartphones Destroyed a Generation?"

5. "Mobile Users Reach to Phone ~150x a Day," *Internet Trends Report 2017*, https://www.slideshare.net/kleiner perkins/kpcb-internet-trends-2013/52-Mobile_Users_ Reach_to_Phone (accessed 3/16/2018).

6. Michael Winnick, "Putting a Finger on Our Phone Obsession," *dscout*, June 16, 2016, https://blog.dscout.com /mobile-touches (accessed 1/18/2018).

7. Ibid.

8. Cooper Pinson, "Is It Time to Walk Away from Our Mobile Devices?" Harvest USA, https://www.harvestusa.org /time-walk-away-mobile-devices (accessed 1/18/2018); Paul Lewis, "'Our Minds Can Be Hijacked': The Tech Insiders Who Fear a Smartphone Dystopia," *The Guardian*, October 6, 2017, https://www.theguardian.com/technology/2017 /oct/05/smartphone-addiction-silicon-valley-dystopia (accessed 1/18/2018).

9. Tristan Harris, "The Binge Breaker," *The Atlantic*, November 2016, https://www.theatlantic.com/magazine/ archive/2016/11/the-binge-breaker/501122 (accessed 1/16/ 2018); Lewis, "'Our Minds Can Be Hijacked'"; Eames Yates, "Here's Why Steve Jobs Never Let His Kids Use an iPad," *Business Insider*, March 4, 2017, http://www.business insider.com/heres-why-steve-jobs-never-let-his-kids-use- ipad-apple-social-media-2017-3 (accessed 1/19/2018).

10. Nicholas Thompson, "Our Minds Have Been Hijacked by Our Phones. Tristan Harris Wants to Rescue Them," *Wired.com*, July 26, 2017, https://www.wired.com/ story/our-minds-have-been-hijacked-by-our-phones-tristan- harris-wants-to-rescue-them(accessed 1/16/2018); Tristan Harris, "How a Handful of Tech Companies Control Bil- lions of Minds Every Day," TED.com, https://www.ted .com/talks/tristan_harris_the_manipulative_tricks_tech_ companies_use_to_capture_your_attention#t-70866 (accessed 1/17/2018); Lewis, "'Our Minds Can Be Hijacked.'"

11. Harris, "The Binge Breaker"; Lewis, "'Our Minds Can Be Hijacked.'"

12. Bill Watterson, *Scientific Progress Goes "Boink"* (Kansas City, MO: Andrews and McMeel, 1991), 119.